D1265938

URBAN WARFARE

SPECIAL FORCES: PROTECTING, BUILDING, TEACHING, AND FIGHTING

AIR FORCE

ARMY RANGERS

ELITE FORCES SELECTION

ESCAPE AND EVASION

GREEN BERETS

MARINES

NAVY SEALS

URBAN WARFARE

PARACHUTE REGIMENT

WORLD'S BEST SOLDIERS

URBAN WARFARE

by Jack Montana

Mason Crest Publishers

MASON CREST PUBLISHERS INC.
370 Reed Road
Broomall, Pennsylvania 19008
(866)MCP-BOOK (toll free)
www.masoncrest.com

First Printing
9 8 7 6 5 4 3 2 1

Library of Congress Cataloging-in-Publication Data

Montana, Jack.
 Urban warfare / by Jack Montana.
    p. cm. — (Special forces: protecting, building, teaching and fighting)
 Includes bibliographical references and index.
 ISBN 978-1-4222-1844-0 ISBN (series) 978-1-4222-1836-5
 1. Urban warfare—Juvenile literature. I. Title.
 U167.5.S7.M66 2011
 355.4'26—dc22
                          2010024704

Produced by Harding House Publishing Service, Inc.
www.hardinghousepages.com
Interior design by MK Bassett-Harvey.
Cover design by Torque Advertising + Design.
Printed in USA by Bang Printing.

With thanks and appreciation to the U.S. Military for the use of information, text, and images.

Contents

Introduction 6

1. The Challenges of Urban Warfare 9

2. The History of Urban Warfare 19

3. Urban Warfare and the U.S. Marines 27

4. Urban Warfare in Iraq 37

5. Overcoming Fear 51

Find Out More on the Internet 59

Further Reading 59

Bibliography 60

Index 62

Picture Credits 63

About the Author and Consultant 64

Introduction

Elite forces are the tip of Freedom's spear. These small, special units are universally the first to engage, whether on reconnaissance missions into denied territory for larger conventional forces or in direct action, surgical operations, preemptive strikes, retaliatory action, and hostage rescues. They lead the way in today's war on terrorism, the war on drugs, the war on transnational unrest, and in humanitarian operations as well as nation building. When large-scale warfare erupts, they offer theater commanders a wide variety of unique, unconventional options.

Most such units are regionally oriented, acclimated to the culture and conversant in the languages of the areas where they operate. Since they deploy to those areas regularly, often for combined training exercises with indigenous forces, these elite units also serve as peacetime "global scouts," and "diplomacy multipliers," beacons of hope for the democratic aspirations of oppressed peoples all over the globe.

Elite forces are truly "quiet professionals": their actions speak louder than words. They are self-motivated, self-confidant, versatile, seasoned, mature individuals who rely on teamwork more than daring-do. Unfortunately, theirs is dangerous work. Since the 1980 attempt to rescue hostages from the U.S. embassy in Tehran, American special operations forces have suffered casualties in real-world operations at close to fifteen times the rate of U.S. conventional forces. By the very nature of the challenges that face special operations forces, training for these elite units has proven even more hazardous.

Thus it's with special pride that I join you in saluting the brave men who volunteer to serve in and support these magnificent units and who face such difficult challenges ahead.

—*Colonel John T. Carney, Jr., USAF–Ret.*
President, Special Operations Warrior Foundation

CHAPTER 1
The Challenges of Urban Warfare

The United States is known for its "BIG" military, meaning that threats to the country are met with big responses, big machinery, and big battalions. Most enemy countries cannot compete with the size and power of the U.S. military because they do not have the monetary or technological means. However, they can bring the battles to areas that remove the U.S. advantage.

In certain types of terrain, the only possible type of combat is small-scale, soldier-to-soldier fighting, which requires very different skills from large-scale battles. In addition, the terrain itself gives an advantage to the opponents because it is their local and familiar area. In past wars, complex terrain with which U.S. soldiers had to contend included jungles and mountains. In today's wars, cities often provide the perfect location for enemies to gain an upper hand over U.S. troops.

CHALLENGES OF THE URBAN TERRAIN

The characteristics of an average city include tall buildings, narrow alleys, sewage tunnels, and possibly a subway system. Defenders may have the advantage of detailed local knowledge of the area, right down to the layout inside of buildings and means of travel not shown on maps. The buildings can provide excellent sniping posts, while alleys and rubble-filled streets are ideal for planting booby traps. Defenders can move from one part of the city to another undetected, using underground tunnels and then springing ambushes. Meanwhile, the attackers tend to become more exposed than the defender as they must use the open streets more often, since they will be unfamiliar with the defenders' secret and hidden routes. During a house-to-house search, the attacker is often also exposed on the streets.

The urban environment is just as complex as a jungle or the mountains, and it provides the opponents with familiar terrain, a supporting population (within which they are able to conceal themselves easily), and an established **infrastructure**. There are a lot of people in an urban combat setting—soldiers must learn to recognize which members of the population pose a threat (combatants) and which are civilians, or noncombatants. The space available for battle

UNDERSTAND THE FULL MEANING

infrastructure: The basic physical and organizational structures and facilities (e.g., buildings, roads, and power supplies) in a society.

Japanese Ground Self Defense Force (JGSDF) soldiers from the 20th Infantry Regiment, armed with Howa 5.56 mm Type 89 assault rifles, demonstrate Military Operations in Urban Terrain (MOUT) techniques in the snow during Exercise Forest Light 2004, conducted in the Ojijibara Maneuver Area of Sendai, Japan. Forest Light is a bi-lateral training exercise conducted between the JGSDF and the U.S. Marine Corps.

is also much smaller in an urban setting. In open battles, there are often thousands of meters between the opposing sides, but in an urban environment this "red zone" can be only tens of meters. The close quarters limit the effectiveness of many types of weapons, make rescue missions more difficult, and lead to more casualties.

Since the end of World War II, four out of five Americans killed in battle have been **infantrymen**. These soldiers make up less than 5 percent of all servicemen, but they do most of the killing and dying. Despite this fact, more time and money is spent in training and equipping pilots (and other "long-distance" fighters) than in preparing the close-combat soldiers. Also, in general, there are fewer soldiers trained for close combat.

The prevailing **doctrine** has been that U.S. **intelligence** and large-battle **tactics** would reduce the enemy's strength enough that the close-combat battles would be small and unimportant. However, this is not the reality—instead, urban battles are becoming the focus of modern campaigns, and urban environments will continue to be an ongoing military challenge for the United States as cities around the world expand and become more densely populated.

UNDERSTAND THE FULL MEANING

infantrymen: Soldiers who fight on foot.

doctrine: A set of beliefs.

intelligence: Information collected by the military.

tactics: Actions or strategies planned to achieve a specific goal.

A Special Forces GI wields his carbine during street fighting in Baghdad.

TRAINING FOR URBAN COMBAT

The specific challenges posed by urban environments require unique training to prepare soldiers for urban combat or for urban-based rescue missions. Military Operations on Urban Terrain training, or MOUT training, uses a number of different techniques to teach soldiers about the obstacles they may face in urban combat.

UNDERSTANDING THE TERRAIN

First, the soldiers must understand what an urban terrain is—what structures they might encounter, how big the area is within which they will be fighting, and what effects warfare has already had on the environment.

Cities are composed of many different features of varying shapes and sizes. The terrain is a combination of overhead airspace; horizontal, vertical, interior, exterior, and **subterranean** forms and surfaces; as well as natural hills and slopes, drainage, and vegetation. All these different spaces and shapes combine to create a complex pattern that is unique to each city. As a result, a city may appear small compared to an open battle space, but all the surfaces and shapes in the city make the overall defensible area of the urban area much larger than an equal-sized portion of undeveloped terrain. In addition, the shape of the overall city, as well as the pattern of street layout, have an effect on urban combat planning and execution.

UNDERSTAND THE FULL MEANING

subterranean: Underground.

Finally, urban operations themselves alter urban environments, something that soldiers must be prepared handle when in the midst of combat. Combat can result in fallen structures, unstable buildings or other structures, power outages, flooding, as well as the release of toxic substances.

TRAINING FACILITIES

The military uses special MOUT training complexes, which are set up to resemble various urban environments. Different branches of the military use these facilities to train soldiers for situations they are most likely to encounter when on active duty.

The Army created an urban operations task force in 1999 to develop an overarching urban operations training strategy. The major focus of the strategy revolves around new facilities designed to provide urban operations training from the individual level up through the battalion level.

The Army MOUT training complex at Ft. McCoy, Wisconsin, is built in a field and contains cars, trucks, deserted buildings, and alleyways. The training consists of three phases: individual training, team training, and finally a live-fire exercise.

The individual phase teaches soldiers how to move in a room, how to communicate with other soldiers, and how to be aware of each other's weapons and lines of sight. During the teamwork phase, soldiers work in teams of four, and move through the "city," concentrating on acting as a single unit, rather than four separate people. The live-fire phase gives the team a chance to enter and clear a room using targets and live rounds.

Pararescuemen practice an urban village assault to extract a downed pilot during a combat search and rescue integration exercise.

The Marine Corps also uses mock cities to conduct urban combat training. Like the Army Forces, the Marines conduct training to prepare for combat situations, but they also participate in other types of tactical training. For example, the Kilo 2 MOUT training facility at Camp Pendleton, California, is set up to resemble an Afghan village, including role players who act like villagers. The soldiers training here are working to prepare for less aggressive urban encounters. "We are learning how to work with the Afghan National Army and the Afghan National Police in order to build up security so that locals will feel safe in their homes," says Lance Corporal Jeffrey Renn, a soldier in training at the facility. In addition, the Marines are learning to communicate and build rapport with locals.

Air Force troops need MOUT training as well. At the Bagram Air Base in Afghanistan, Air Force security forces train for rescue missions using the Army's MOUT training facility at Bagram. As the trainees move through the mock village, high-tech cameras record every moment. The videos are then used to provide the soldiers with feedback on their training progress.

At every MOUT training facility, no matter the specific situation being trained for, the focus of training is on preparing to work in this new combat environment and learning to operate as a single small team, instead of as individuals who are part of a large platoon. "It's harder than it looks, everyone has to be on the same page," said Private Kavon Ford, after training at the Army's Malone MOUT training facility in Fort Benning, Georgia. "Teamwork is the most difficult part. Learning to count on my teammates makes my job easier."

CHAPTER 2
The History of Urban Warfare

Urban warfare is a growing concern for the modern U.S. military, but it is not a new issue. The United States has fought in urban settings in previous operations. For example, World War II saw many battles waged in the cities of Europe and Asia.

The Battle of Manila, in the Pacific **theater**, was a battle fought by U.S., Filipino, and Japanese forces in the capital of the Philippines. The battle lasted a month, from February to March of 1945, and in that month the city was devastated. Japanese forces had occupied many cities in Southeast Asia

UNDERSTAND THE FULL MEANING

theater: The large geographic area where military operations are taking place.

during the war, but Manila was the only one to see battle—the Japanese surrendered other cities without a fight. In Manila, the leader of the U.S. forces, General Douglas MacArthur ordered U.S. forces to move quickly toward the city, leaving the Japanese little time to evacuate, and General Tomoyuki Yamashita, the Japanese commander, did not evacuate in the little time he had.

Despite being outnumbered, Japanese forces managed to wage an effective defense against the American attack. Initially, in an effort to protect civilian lives, MacArthur wanted to restrict the use of heavy artillery or attack from the air. However, the effectiveness of the Japanese defenses eventually forced the use of major artillery, which contributed to the destruction of the city and the deaths of 100,000 civilians.

BATTLE IN BERLIN

The Russians did a lot to develop urban warfare tactics during the Second World War. During the Battle of Berlin, a Soviet combat group, a mixed-arms unit of about eighty men, divided into assault groups of six to eight men, closely supported by field artillery. These units were able to apply the tactics of house-to-house fighting that the Soviets had already been forced to develop and refine at each *festung stadt* (fortress city) they had encountered in their march from Stalingrad to Berlin.

Meanwhile, the Germans tactics used for the urban warfare that took place in Berlin was dictated by three considerations: the experience the Germans had gained during five years of war; the physical characteristics of Berlin; and the tactics used by the Soviets.

Most of Berlin's central districts were city blocks with straight wide roads, and included several waterways, parks, and a large railway marshalling yard. It was predominantly flat, but there were some low hills. Much of the housing stock consisted of apartment blocks built in the second half of the nineteenth century, most of which were five stories high and built around a courtyard that could be reached from the street through a corridor large enough to drive a horse

This photograph shows the destruction left in a Berlin street after the Battle of Berlin in 1945.

and cart or the small trucks used to deliver coal. In many places, these apartment blocks were built around several courtyards, one behind the other, each one reached through the outer courtyards by a ground-level tunnel similar to that between the first courtyard and the road. The larger, more expensive apartments faced the street and the smaller less expensive ones could be found around the inner courtyards.

Just as the Soviets had learned a lot about urban warfare, so had the Germans. The German forces did not use make-shift barricades erected close to street corners, because these could be raked by artillery fire from guns firing over open sights further along the straight streets. Instead, they put snipers and machine guns on the upper floors and the roofs because the Soviet tanks could not elevate their guns that high. The Germans put armed men in cellar windows to ambush tanks as they moved down the streets.

To counter these tactics, the Soviets mounted sub-machine gunners on the tanks. The gunners sprayed every doorway and window, but this meant the tank could not **traverse** its **turret** quickly. The other solution was to rely on heavy **howitzers** firing over open sights to blast defended buildings and to use anti-aircraft guns against the German gunners on the higher floors.

UNDERSTAND THE FULL MEANING

traverse: To turn a gun to make it point in any required direction.

turret: A domelike armored structure containing mounted guns and able to turn in order to aim in different directions.

howitzers: Relatively short-barreled cannons used to fire rounds at a high angle, reaching behind barricades or into trenches.

Soviet combat groups started to move from house to house instead of directly down the streets. They moved through the apartments and cellars, blasting holes through the walls of adjacent buildings, while others fought across the roof tops and through the attics. These tactics caught the Germans off guard, as they lay in ambush for tanks. Flamethrowers and grenades were very effective, but as the Berlin civilian population had not been evacuated, these tactics inevitably killed many civilians. Urban warfare is dangerous for civilians!

FIRST CHECHEN WAR

During the First Chechen War in the 1990s, most of the Chechen fighters had been trained in the Soviet armed forces, so they were well-trained for the urban warfare they encountered. In the battles that took place in city streets, they were divided into combat groups consisting of fifteen to twenty personnel, subdivided into three or four-man fire teams. A fire team consisted of an antitank gunner, usually armed with Russian-made weapons, a machine gunner, and a sniper. Ammunition runners and assistant gunners supported the team.

To destroy Russian armored vehicles in the city of Grozny, five or six hunter-killer fire teams deployed at ground level, in second and third stories, and in basements. The snipers and machine gunners would pin down the supporting infantry while the antitank gunners would engage the armored vehicle aiming at the top, rear, and sides of vehicles.

At first, the Russians were taken by surprise. Their armored columns that were supposed to take the city without difficulty in the same way Soviet forces had taken Budapest in 1956 were decimated instead. Using the experience they'd learned in Berlin, as a short term measure they deployed self-propelled anti-aircraft guns to engage the Chechen combat groups, as their tank's main gun did not have the elevation and depression to engage the fire teams and an armored vehicle's machine gun could not suppress the fire of half a dozen different fire teams simultaneously. In the long term, the Russians brought in more infantry and began a systematic advance through the city, house by house and block by block, with dismounted Russian infantry moving in support of armor. In proactive moves, the Russians started to set up ambush points of their own and then move units toward them to lure the Chechen combat groups into ambushes.

Humanitarian Urban Operations

The MOUT training U.S. special forces receive may not always be applied in combat situations. After the 7.0 earthquake that ravaged Haiti in January of 2010, special Air Force urban search and rescue teams were deployed for humanitarian relief efforts on the island nation.

Airmen worked with California Task Force 2, a highly-trained Federal Emergency Management Agency (FEMA) team made up of doctors, paramedics, structural specialists, rescue members, and dogs trained to search for humans amongst the rubble of destroyed buildings.

California Task Force 2 has been active for twenty years, and has worked to provide humanitarian aid after disasters like the 2004 Southeast Asia tsunami.

In Berlin in 1945, some of the Soviet tanks had attached bedsprings to the outside of their turrets to reduce the damage done by German fire—and now, in Chechnya, some of the Russian armored vehicles were fitted quickly with a cage of wire mesh.

Today, military recruits still study these historical examples of urban warfare, learning all they can from the lessons of the past. But there is still more to learn.

Ron Wickbacher, along with his dog, Dawson, prepare to load onto a C-17 Globemaster III on their way to Haiti on January 14, 2010. Mr. Wickbacher is a canine search specialist from California Task Force 2, and Dawson is a live-scent dog trained for humanitarian search and rescue.

CHAPTER 3
Urban Warfare and the U.S. Marines

On a winter day in January 2009, residents of Richmond, Virginia, wondered if war had broken out in their streets.

No, it hadn't. But war games had. About 2,200 Marines from Camp Lejeune, North Carolina, were undergoing more than two weeks of urban warfare training in the Richmond area. Using Fort Pickett as a base for their operations, the Marines underwent realistic urban training exercise to prepare them for future conflicts.

A NEED FOR MORE TRAINING

In 2004, in the U.S. Marine Corps' *Proceedings*, Major Kelly P. Houlgate had emphasized the U.S. Marines' need for increased training in urban warfare. The training in Richmond was just one part of the Marines' increased emphasis on urban warfare.

Major Houlgate reminded the Marines that by 2020 about 85 percent of the world's inhabitants will be crowded into coastal cities—cities that will often lack the infrastructure required to support their growing populations. Under these conditions, Major Houlgate pointed out, ethnic and economic tensions will simmer and possibly explode, requiring U.S. intervention.

Of the twenty-six conflicts in which the Marines fought since the 1980s, twenty-one involved some urban fighting, and ten relied completely on urban warfare tactics. The Marines' experience in Lebanon, Panama, Khafji, Somalia, Liberia, and the Balkans all demonstrated the need to be able to conduct a wide array of operations in close terrain. As the global war on terrorism continued, the Marines knew they would need to focus on fighting and winning in urban areas. Instead of having to relearn the lessons of urban warfare each time they encountered a new situation, they needed to be prepared.

PREPARING FOR URBAN WARFARE

Urban warfare considerations began to drive decision-making in all administrative areas, from acquisitions to manpower. Vehicles, aircraft, logistics equipment, communications systems, and weapons needed to be procured with an emphasis on what the equipment could do in an urban

Marine Regiment, Third Marine Division, practice Military Operations and Urban Terrain (MOUT) warfare at the Camp Hansen, Central Training Area, using unarmed safety rigged Colt 5.56mm M16A2 Assault Rifles.

Soldiers from the 82nd Airborne Division's, First Battalion, 325th Infantry Regiment, show Egyptian and Pakistani soldiers how to properly enter a room during MOUT training at the Mubarak Military City, Egypt, during Operation Bright Star. The training was part of the overall exercise designed to build partnerships and military cooperation between the eleven countries involved in the exercise.

environment. In the same way that the Marines have always bought equipment with a focus on weight and size (because of airlift and **amphibious** considerations), now the Marines needed equipment with an urban-warfare focus.

The Marine Corps needed to make a significant investment in urban combat training facilities. It needed large training facilities both in the continental United States and overseas, facilities that included large, fenced-off, live-fire zones with realistic and rapidly repairable structures that would allow for combined small-arms air-artillery live-fire training. The portions of these new training facilities for maneuver and long-term operations would incorporate numerous types of construction to represent various regions of the world. Opposition forces would be established at each facility to act as a consistent, thinking enemy. When units were not engaged with a thinking, moving enemy, they would fight simulated, computerized foes.

Squads of Marines would begin to train on interactive video screens, working to develop their urban decision-making and fighting skills with instant feedback. These urban video games were modern versions of games such as Marine Doom. Older Marines sometimes shuddered at the thought of training in front of a television or computer monitor—but experts believed these game would sharpen soldiers' urban warfare skills.

In the past, special training centers have prepared Marines for particular kinds of fighting, such as mountain

UNDERSTAND THE FULL MEANING

amphibious: Able to be used both on land and in water.

warfare. In the twenty-first century, the Marines now needs special centers to prepare them for urban combat.

Historically, the Corps has "made Marines" at its entry-level schools by imbuing men and women with the Marines' culture—but experts believe it needs to have an expanded emphasis on urban warfare. History classes in entry-level schools should be updated to emphasize urban combat. While the Corps should not ignore its World War II heritage, training videos should emphasize the battles at Fallujah, as they now do Tarawa and Iwo Jima. Military occupational specialty schools other than just School of Infantry and Infantry Officers' Course would train using urban warfare procedures and techniques. Marine recruits need to expect to deal with urban warfare once they graduate.

In the twenty-first-century Marine Corps, the term "urban warfare" must become a common expression. Commanders will teach their Marines about the Corps' urban heritage. Just as "expeditionary forward **deployment** on amphibious ships" is simply part of the Marines' identity, urban combat must now take on a similar status within the Marines.

RISING TO THE CHALLENGE

Before World War II, the United States needed an amphibious armed force, capable of fighting with equal skill on land and on water. The U.S. Marines rose to the challenge.

UNDERSTAND THE FULL MEANING

deployment: The process of sending troops into a specific area of a battle zone.

U.S. Marine Corps Lance Corporal (LCPL) Daniel Soto, assigned to F/ Company, Second Battalion, Sixth Marine Regiment, Second Marine Division, readies his 5.56 mm M249 Squad Automatic Weapon (SAW), as he observes the movement of opposing forces, during a MOUT demonstration conducted during Exercise Forest Light 2004, in the snow covered Ojojibara Maneuver Area of Sendai, Japan.

And they must do so again, rising to the challenge of urban warfare.

Major Houlgate suggests that the Marine Corps should address safety concerns in three ways:

- By studying and perhaps revising live-fire safety regulations. The sharpest minds of Marine Corps safety, marksmanship, and training should convene to re-examine current safety systems, policies, and procedures. All units should increase the use of operational risk management to reduce risks and closely examine training procedures.

- By developing a specific urban training standard operating procedure that will apply Corps-wide. In addition, urban warfare lessons learned from Iraq, reflecting real-world use of the latest weapon systems, needs to be incorporated into safety regulations and urban standard operating procedure.

- By developing training munitions that will foster more realistic and safer combined-arms training. Thin-skinned paint-filled or water-filled "bombs" and "shells" should be developed. Research should increase toward finding viable munitions such as "deadened" bullets that expend their energy more

UNDERSTAND THE FULL MEANING

guerrillas: Small groups of fighters who use tactics such as ambushes, raids, and sabotage.

innovation: Something new and different that has been introduced.

rapidly and grenades that stun temporarily and without physical damage to training personnel. The goal
of the new training munitions should be maximizing
safety and feedback.

According to Major Houlgate, those who say that "if it
ain't broke, don't fix it" need to be reminded that the Marines
were not broken in the 1920s and 1930s. In the years before
World War II, the Marines were busy—and successful—in the
Caribbean nations fighting guerrillas. Innovation and
change do not necessarily occur because there is a fundamental problem; instead, they should occur *before* there is
a fundamental problem. Combat in Fallujah and other Iraqi
cities has proved the Marines' need for urban warfare excel-
lence.

Meanwhile, the Marines' goal remains unchanged: to win
America's wars.

CHAPTER 4

Urban Warfare in Iraq

Throughout the war in Iraq, Special Forces and the rest of the U.S. military have been called on to fight in urban battles. The city of Fallujah proved to be one of the most challenging urban sites of all.

THE FIRST BATTLE OF FALLUJAH

BACKGROUND

Fallujah had generally benefited economically under Saddam Hussein, and many residents were employed as police, military and intelligence officers by his administration. However, there was little sympathy for Saddam after the collapse of his government, which many residents had considered to be oppressive. The city was one of the most religious and culturally traditional areas in Iraq.

After the collapse of the previous infrastructure in early 2003, local residents had elected a town council led by Taha Bidaywi Hamed, who kept the city from falling into the control of looters and common criminals. The town council and Hamed were both considered to be nominally pro-American. At first, the United States assumed that their election meant that the city would be unlikely to become an area of dangerous tension. Few American troops were sent to Fallujah as a result.

Gradually, however, tensions grew in Fallujah, along with a growing anti-American sentiment. U.S. forces were called in to deal with anti-American protests, and shots were exchanged. Eventually, forces from the Third Armored Cavalry Regiment and 101st Airborne Division replaced the Eighty-Second Airborne troops, and on June 4 the Third Armored Cavalry was forced to request an additional 1,500 troops to help quell the growing resistance they faced in Fallujah.

Then at the end of June 2003, an explosion occurred in a mosque, killing the **imam** and eight other people. The local population claimed that Americans had fired a missile at the mosque, while the U.S. forces said the explosion had been an accidental detonation by **insurgents** constructing bombs. Tensions in the city were now at a boiling point.

UNDERSTAND THE FULL MEANING

imam: A Muslim religious leader in charge of a mosque.

insurgents: Rebels; those who take up arms against the established leadership.

THE OUTBREAK OF FIGHTING

On February 12, 2004, insurgents attacked a convoy carrying General John Abizaid, the commander of U.S. Forces in the Middle East, and the Eighty-second Airborne's Major General Charles Swannack, firing on the vehicles from nearby rooftops. Eleven days later, insurgents diverted Iraqi police to a false emergency on the outskirts of the city, before

The cost of urban warfare is always high, since the fighting takes place among buildings that are people's homes and businesses. Much of the city of Fallujah was left in ruins after the battles.

simultaneously attacking three police stations, the mayor's office, and a civil defense base. At least seventeen police officers were killed.

Meanwhile, the Eighty-second Airborne were conducting regular "lightning raids" inside the city, using convoys to destroy road barriers and curbs that could hide IEDs, and overseeing searches of homes and schools.

By early March 2004, the city began to fall under the increasing influence of guerrilla factions. The rising violence against the American presence resulted in the complete withdrawal of troops from the city, with only occasional incursions to try to regain a foothold in the city.

THE BLACKWATER KILLINGS

On March 31, 2004, Iraqi insurgents in Fallujah ambushed a convoy containing four American private military contractors from Blackwater USA who were making food deliveries. Machine gun fire and a grenade thrown through a window of their SUV killed the four armed contractors, Scott Helvenston, Jerko Zovko, Wesley Batalona, and Michael Teague. A mob then set their bodies ablaze, and their corpses were dragged through the streets. Photos of the event were released to news agencies worldwide, causing indignation and moral outrage in the United States.

Until now, the Marine Corps had been maintaining a strategy of foot patrols, less aggressive raids, humanitarian aid, and close cooperation with local leaders. This approach

UNDERSTAND THE FULL MEANING

IEDs: Improvised Explosive Devices.

was suspended now, and a military operation was set in motion to clear guerrillas from Fallujah.

THE BATTLE

On April 1, Brigadier General Mark Kimmitt, deputy director of operations for the U.S. military in Iraq, promised an "overwhelming" response to the Blackwater deaths, stating "We will pacify that city." On the night of April 4, the U.S. forces launched a major assault by encircling the city with about 2000 troops. Sporadic gunfire went on throughout the night.

By the morning of April 5, American units had surrounded the city, headed by the 1st Marine Expeditionary Force. American troops blockaded roads leading into the city with Humvees and concertina wire. They also took over a local radio station and handed out leaflets urging residents to remain inside their homes and help American forces identify insurgents and any Fallujans who were involved in the Blackwater deaths. Up to a third of the civilian population fled the city.

The rebels in Fallujah held on as the Americans tightened their noose on the city. Air bombardments rained on insurgent positions throughout the city, and Lockheed AC-130 gunships attacked targets with their Gatling guns and howitzers. Scout Snipers became a core element of the Marines' strategy, while PSYOP Tactical Psychological Operations Teams tried to lure Iraqis out into the open for the Scout Snipers by reading scripts that were aimed at angering insurgent fighters; they also blared Hell's Bells by AC/DC over their loud speakers, along with music by other rock groups, such as Metallica.

After three days of fighting, it was estimated that the United States had gained control over about a quarter of the city, and the insurgents had lost a number of key defensive positions. But the U.S. attacks were taking a toll on civilians as well as the insurgents. About six hundred Iraqis had been killed, at least half of whom were non-combatants.

At noon on April 9, an announcement was made that the U.S. forces would be **unilaterally** holding a ceasefire, to facilitate negotiations between the Iraqi Governing Council, insurgents, and city spokespersons, and to allow government supplies to be delivered to residents. Much-needed humanitarian relief, which had been held up by the fighting and blockade, finally managed to enter the city, notably a major convoy organized by private citizens, businessmen, and clerics from Baghdad as a joint Shi'a-Sunni effort.

Although hundreds of insurgents had been killed in the assault, the city remained firmly in their control. U.S. forces had by then only managed to gain a foothold in the industrial district to the south of the city. The end of major operations for the time being led to negotiations between various Iraqi elements and the Coalition forces, punctuated by occasional firefights. Finally, on April 27, insurgents attacked U.S. defensive positions, forcing Americans to call in air support.

UNDERSTAND THE FULL MEANING

unilaterally: Referring to something that is done by one side or person only.

On May 1, 2004, the United States withdrew from Fallujah, as Lieutenant General James Conway announced that he had unilaterally decided to turn over any remaining operations to the newly-formed Fallujah Brigade, which would be armed with U.S. weapons and equipment. Unfortunately, this group dissolved and turned over all the U.S. weapons to the insurgency.

THE SECOND BATTLE OF FALLUJAH: OPERATION PHANTOM FURY

The U.S. forces knew they would have to go back into Fallujah. So they began to prepare for another round of urban warfare.

PREPARATION

Before beginning their attack, U.S. and Iraqi forces established checkpoints around Fallujah to prevent anyone from entering the city and to intercept insurgents attempting to flee. In addition, overhead imagery was used to prepare maps of the city for use by the attackers. Iraqi interpreters helped American troops get ready for the planned fight. After weeks of withstanding air strikes and artillery bombardment, the militants holed up in the city appeared to be vulnerable to direct attack. It was time to use urban warfare tactics.

THE BATTLE

Ground operations began on the night of November 7, 2004. Attacking from the west and south, the Iraqi Thirty-Sixth

U.S. Marines fight in the city of Fallujah during Operation Phantom Fury/Operation Al Fajr (New Dawn).

Commando Battalion, with their U.S. Army Special Forces advisers, and the U.S. Marine Corps 3rd Light Armored Reconnaissance Battalion, reinforced by Bravo Company from the Marine Corp Reserve's 1st Battalion, Twenty-third Regiment, and supported by Combat Service Support Company 113, from Combat Service Support Battalion 1, captured Fallujah General Hospital and villages opposite the Euphrates River along Fallujah's western edge. The same unit, operating under the command of the U.S. Army III Corps, then moved on the western approaches to the city, securing the Jurf Kas Sukr Bridge. These initial attacks, however, were little more than a diversion, intended to distract and confuse the rebels defending the city.

Navy Seabees from NMCB-23 shut off electrical power at the substation located just northeast of the city, and then two Marine Regimental Combat Teams, Regimental Combat Team 1 and Regimental Combat Team 7, launched their attack along the northern edge of the city. Two U.S. Army heavy battalion-sized units, the Second Squadron, 7 Cavalry Regiment, and Second Battalion, Second Infantry Regiment were also in place. These two battalions were to be followed by four infantry battalions that would clear the buildings. The Army's mechanized Second Brigade, First Cavalry Division, helped by the Marine's Second Reconnaissance Battalion would surround the city. The British Black Watch Battalion patrolled the main highways to the east. Everything was in place.

The six battalions of Army-Marine-Iraqi forces, moving under the cover of darkness, began the assault in the early hours of November 8, 2004, with an intense bombing, followed by an attack on the main train station. By that afternoon, under the protection of intense air cover, Marines had entered the Hay Naib al-Dubat and al-Naziza districts of the city. The Marines were followed in by the Navy Seabees of NMCB-4 who bulldozed the streets clear of debris from the bombardment that morning. Shortly after nightfall on November 9, 2004, the Marines were along Highway 10 in the center of the city. While most of the fighting subsided by November 13, 2004, Marines continued to face determined resistance from the enemy in and around the city.

By November 16, 2004, after nine days of fighting, the Marine command described the action as mopping up pockets of resistance. Sporadic fighting continued until December 23, 2004. The Marines had won the day.

By late January 2005, news reports indicated U.S. combat units were leaving the area and were helping the local population to return to the heavily-damaged city. The U.S. Army's Second Battalion, Second Infantry Regiment was awarded the Presidential Unit Citation for actions during the battle. Additionally, Operation Phantom Fury yielded a nominee for the Medal of Honor, Sergeant Rafael Peralta who was a Marine with First Battalion, Third Marines. Sergeant Peralta was later awarded the Navy Cross, the second highest award a Marine can receive.

But urban warfare is costly. Fallujah suffered extensive damage to residences, mosques, city services, and businesses. The city, once referred to as the "City of Mosques," had once had more than two hundred mosques—more than

A U.S. Marine Corps Marine M1A1 Abrams Main Battle Tank, 2nd Tank Battalion, fires its main gun into a building to provide suppressive counter fire against insurgents who fired on other Marines during a fire fight in Fallujah, Al Anbar Province, Iraq. These Marines are participating in Operation Al Fajr, an offensive operation conducted against Iraqi insurgent forces as part of a Security and Stabilization Operation (SASO) carried out during Operation Iraqi Freedom.

Special Forces in Urban Warfare

U.S. special forces have played a key role in the global fight against terrorism—though mostly a secret one. As a result, when the number of American troops in Iraq were reduced in 2010, the level of U.S. special operations forces in Iraq remained the same.

As part of their training, and through their experiences, these soldiers have learned that urban and unconventional warfare is becoming more important in America's defense.

In addition to direct combat and counterterrorism, special operations forces—among them Army Green Berets, Navy SEALs, Air Force special operations personnel and Marine operators—conduct an array of indirect missions. These include psychological operations and the training and support of paramilitary forces to help achieve U.S. aims, such as when special operations forces partnered with the Northern Alliance to undermine the Taliban in Afghanistan before the American invasion began in earnest in 2001.

"The United States Special Operations Command deliberately leans forward to ensure that proper resources and tools are being applied in these regions. We call it 'Being ahead of the sound of guns,'" said Navy Adm. Eric Olson, the first Navy SEAL to ascend to a four-star officer rank. "As proud as we are of our ability to respond quickly to gunfire when it occurs," he continued, "we are at least as proud of our ability . . . to prevent that sound ultimately from occurring in places that are at risk."

sixty had been destroyed in the fighting. Many of these mosques had been used as arms caches and weapon strong points by Islamist forces. Perhaps half the homes in the city suffered at least some damage. Of the roughly 50,000 buildings in Fallujah, between 7,000 and 10,000 were estimated to have been destroyed in the offensive and from half to two-thirds of the remaining buildings had notable damage. As many as six thousand civilians were said to have died during the fighting.

The recapture of the city, however, proved to be largely a success for U.S. forces, with a large number of local insurgent fighters killed. In the face of overwhelming U.S. firepower, the momentum of the Sunni rebellion was slowed. Furthermore, al-Qaeda's foothold in Iraq had been seriously weakened. All of this was thanks to the successful urban tactics of the U.S. forces.

CHAPTER 5

Overcoming Fear

Soldiers fighting in urban warfare must be able to handle fear. The situation is dangerous, and their very lives depend on them being able to stay calm and alert. The lessons that they learn in this situation apply to your life as well. You may not be faced with city streets filled with enemy gunfire—but real-life challenges can be just as terrifying sometimes.

Fear is a very natural response to being attacked, and everyone feels it. People who say that they are frightened of nothing are fooling themselves. Special forces see fear as a positive emotion. However, it is possible to become **immobilized** by fear, and it is this response that enemy troops

UNDERSTAND THE FULL MEANING

immobilized: Put out of action.

51

CONTROLLING FEAR WHEN PARACHUTING

The Air Force Special Operations Command's pararescuemen (PJs) are elite soldiers, yet even they may feel fear when they jump out of an airplane. The act of jumping from thousands of feet in the air is frightening and seems to go against natural logic. In addition, PJs are often jumping down into perilous situations. These elite soldiers know the risks, and may feel fear, but they jump because of their training. They do not want to let their fellow soldiers down, and they do not want to let themselves down. Through successful training, all fears can be overcome and controlled.

seek in their victims. Society's attitude often regards fear as a negative emotion, but the opposite is true. Fear can help fighting troops if they can control it and use it in their defense.

When you are frightened, the **adrenal glands** release **adrenaline** into the bloodstream. The effect of this is that, for a short time at least, the body can summon inner reserves of energy and strength. It is the equivalent of a turbo charger in a car. People can run faster and lift heavier weights, and their sense are sharpened—eyesight, hearing, and the senses of smell, touch, and taste. This is a survival mechanism that all animals have, including humans, and it is the basis of the **fight-or-flight response** to stress.

The danger in a combat situation is that troops may lose control of all this useful energy and descend into panic, so they have to learn how to coordinate these emergency powers. This is partly a question of focusing the mind on the task at hand. Most people, including elite soldiers, can perform amazing acts of courage or strength in a tense situation that would otherwise have been beyond them. That is the power of adrenaline. In urban warfare situations, soldiers have to perform efficiently using their adrenaline. Focusing, a sense of timing, and basic training—these all come together to help them make the most of their fear.

LEARNING TO BREATHE

One way to exert control over what is happening is to use a breathing technique. Troops inhale through their nose, and concentrate on a point an inch or so beneath their navel for a count of five. They retain the breath for a further five seconds, and then exhale through the mouth. They try to repeat the cycle if they have time. This helps them to use

UNDERSTAND THE FULL MEANING

adrenal glands: A pair of organs situated near the kidneys; these glands produce adrenaline.

adrenaline: Also called epinephrine, this is a chemical released into the body by the adrenal glands. Adrenaline is the body's defense mechanism to pain and/or fear.

fight-or-flight response: The body's response to a dangerous situation, which readies one either to resist forcibly or to run away.

A member of the U.S. Army Special Forces in shown here on a mission to capture terrorists of an insurgent force. Controlling the body's fear reactions is important on a mission like this.

their adrenaline reflexes—something they can call upon when faced with a life or death situation.

By controlling breathing and focusing on what is happening as the adrenaline flows, elite soldiers can work out what to do next and take action. If they are going into a sequence of strikes for which they have trained, they focus on where each strike will land. At the same time, soldiers need to remain as relaxed as possible, to avoid their muscles tightening up and becoming too tense. This will only hamper their efforts.

LEARNING TO LOSE

Many people are reluctant to fight, not only because they do not want to be hurt, but also because they are frightened of losing. However, it is important for soldiers to learn how to lose before they learn how to win. This is where their training comes in. If they are used to simulating fights with training partners, they will gradually lose the fear of defeat that could **paralyze** them in a real-life combat situation.

COPING WITH PAIN

All people are understandably frightened of pain, yet pain is natural and useful, and it prevents soldiers from damaging their bodies with unwise actions. Pain tells soldiers that

UNDERSTAND THE FULL MEANING

paralyze: Render unable to move or speak.

The Marines and Army Special Forces Are Leaders in Close-Quarters Combat Training

The Marine Corps and the Army are the leaders among the services in teaching troops hand-to-hand combat and martial arts skills.

Marines' martial arts training features "a blend of proven disciplines including judo, karate and jujitsu, and bayonet and knife-fighting techniques," said 1st Lt. Jesse L. Sjoberg, Bristol's deputy.

Bristol, who has 35 years of martial arts experience, said the training is necessary because of changing world events. Bristol said the martial arts program integrates three warrior disciplines:

- Mental discipline: The development of the combat mindset and the study of the art of war.

- Character discipline: The firm integration of ethics, values, integrity, and leadership.

- Physical discipline, comprised of fighting techniques with rifle and bayonet, bladed weapons, weapons of opportunity (stick, club, gun), and unarmed combat; combative conditioning—the ability to fight while fatigued in a combat environment; and combat sports—boxing, wrestling, and wooden trainer bayonet fighting.

The program develops confidence not only in individual Marine combat skills, Bristol said, "but also in the skills of your fellow Marines," because battlefield combat requires teamwork. Marines who learn lethal combat skills are expected—and required—to use them responsibly, he said.

Army recruits en route to become infantrymen at Fort Benning, Georgia, get fifteen hours of hand-to-hand combat instruction over fourteen weeks. Troops attending the post's elite Ranger School, and Army Special Forces students at Fort Bragg, North Carolina, receive extensive hand-to-hand combat training—about 30–40 hours over the period of one year.

After troops graduate from initial Special Forces training and are assigned to their operational groups, they undergo additional, specialized hand-to-hand combative training, tailored to the mission needs of each unit.

The Navy and Air Force also provide hand-to-hand and martial arts training, but normally only for members of special operations and law enforcement units.

something is wrong so that they can do something about it. Without pain, the body would accept damaging burns and wounds. Soldiers are trained to understand the function of pain. They can then go on to conquer their fear of it. Pain and fear go together in many ways, and both can be overcome. In a fight, when adrenaline is flowing, the body can temporarily **suppress** pain. In combat, people who have

UNDERSTAND THE FULL MEANING

suppress: Put down by authority or force.

suffered broken limbs, been stabbed, or even shot, often do not notice until after the fight. The pain starts only when the adrenaline levels drop. Only then will soldiers become aware of their injuries.

BE PROACTIVE

The U.S. Army Ranger manual states, "Two of the gravest general dangers to survival are a desire for comfort and a passive outlook." In other words, accept the situation where you find yourself. Don't whine about it. Don't waste energy wishing yourself somewhere else. Instead, face what lies in front of you—and take action! Be **proactive**. Don't wait for someone to save you. Do whatever it takes to change the situation. Trust in your own ability to get yourself through the fear and discomfort—to the other side, where you are the victor!

UNDERSTAND THE FULL MEANING

proactive: Preparing for a situation in advance; being prepared and ready and taking control of a situation.

FIND OUT MORE ON THE INTERNET

Air Force www.airforce.com

Army Recruiting www.goarmy.com

Department of Defense www.defense.gov

Marine Corps www.marines.com

Navy www.navy.com

U.S. Naval Academy www.usna.edu

West Point www.usma.edu

The websites listed on this page were active at the time of publication. The publisher is not responsible for websites that have changed their address or discontinued operation since the date of publication. The publisher will review and update the websites upon each reprint.

FURTHER READING

Benson, Ragnar. *Ragnar's Urban Survival*. Boulder, Colo.: Paladin Press, 2000.

Department of Defense. *Urban Operations Plus Combatives.* Washington, D.C.: Pentagon Publishing, 2010.

Department of Defense. *Urban Operations: US Army*. Washington, D.C.: Pentagon Publishing, 2008.

Iverson, Steven S. *Unarmed Combat: A Manual of Self-Defense, Groundfighting, & Joint Locks.* Colorado Springs, Col.: Spartan Submissions, Inc, 2003.

Joes, Anthony James. *Urban Guerilla Warfare*. Lexington, Ky.: The University Press of Kentucky, 2007.

Shillingford, Ron. *The Elite Forces Handbook of Unarmed Combat*. London: Amber Books, 2000.

BIBILIOGRAPHY

Gilmore, Gerry J. "Marines, Army Lead in Close-Quarters Combat Training," www.defense.gov/news/newsarticle.aspx?id=45845 (10 June 2010).

Kruzel, John J. "Special Forces to Remain in Iraq Through Drawdown," www.centcom.mil/en/news/special-forces-to-remain-in-iraq-through-drawdown.html (11 June 2010).

Kulper, Lance Cpl. Jahn R. "Inside the Mind of a Suicide Bomber," www.quantico.usmc.mil/Sentry/StoryView.aspx?SID=3111 (10 June 2010).

PBS.org, "The Battle for Manila (February–March, 1945)," www.pbs.org/wgbh/amex/macarthur/peopleevents/pandeAMEX98.html (9 June 2010).

Scales, Major General Robert H. "Urban Warfare: A Soldier's View," *Military Review,* January-February, 2005: 9–18.

Trapp, Pfc. Brian. "Soldiers fight through Malone MOUT, Sand Hill men tackle tactics of modern battlefield," www.tradoc.army.mil/pao/training_closeup/MaloneMOUT.htm (9 June 2010).

United States Air Force, "Airmen deliver urban search, rescue team to Haiti," www.af.mil/news/story.asp?id=123185761 (9 June 2010).

_____, "Security forces at Bagram practice urban warfare," www. af.mil/news/story.asp?id=123020164 (8 June 2010).

United States Army, "Combined Arms MOUT Task Force/Integrated MOUT Training System (CAMTF/IMTS)," www.peostri.army.mil/PM-TRADE/mout.jsp (8 June 2010).

_____, "Infantrymen of 178th take on urban terrain," www.mccoy. army.mil/vtriad_online/07252003/MOUT.htm (8 June 2010).

_____, "Soldiers Complete Urban Combat Training," www.army.mil/-news/2008/03/13/7911-soldiers-complete-urban-combat-training/ (8 June 2010).

_____, "Urban Operations," rdl.train.army.mil/soldierPortal/atia/adlsc/view/public/11645-1/fm/3-06/TOC.HTM (7 June 2010).

United States Department of Defense, "Urban Warfare, Jointness Raise New Challenges for Rescue," osd.dtic.mil/news/Sep2004/n09142004_2004091403.html (8 June 2010).

United States Marine Corps, "2/1 Marines take new approach to military operations in urban terrain," www.usmc.mil/unit/imef/Pages/21MarinestakenewapproachtoMOUT.aspx (8 June 2010).

INDEX

adrenaline 52–53, 55, 57–58
Afghanistan 16–17, 48
amphibious 31–32

Battle of Manila 19–20
Berlin 20–21, 23–25
Blackwater 40–41

Chechen War 23–25

Fallujah 32, 35, 37
fear 51–53, 55, 57–58

Germany 20, 22–23, 25
Green Berets 48
guerrillas 34–35 , 40–41

Haiti 24–25
humanitarianism 6, 24–25, 40, 42

infantry 11, 12, 23–24, 32, 45–46, 57
Iraq 34–35, 37, 39–43, 45, 47–49

Manila 19–20
Marines 11, 16–17, 27–28, 31–32, 34–35, 40–41, 45–48, 56–57
Military Operations on Urban Terrain (MOUT) training 11, 14–17, 24

Navy 45–46, 48, 57
    SEALS 48

pain 53, 55, 57–58
parachuting 52

Russia 20, 23–25

search and rescue 16, 24–25
Soviets 20–25

terrain 9–10, 14, 28
terrorism 6, 28, 48

World War II 12, 19–20, 32, 35

PICTURE CREDITS

ABOUT THE AUTHOR

Jack Montana lives in upstate New York with his wife and three dogs. He writes on military survival, health, and wellness. He graduated from Binghamton University.

ABOUT THE CONSULTANT

Colonel John Carney, Jr. is USAF-Retired, President and the CEO of the Special Operations Warrior Foundation.